MONSTERS CAN MOSEY

Understanding Shades of Meaning

by Gillia M. Olson

illustrated by Ivica Stevanovic

PICTURE WINDOW BOOKS

a capstone imprint

"Bye, Uncle Rob!" Frankie yelled.

"Bye, Fran-keeeee," said Uncle Rob in his usual zombie drone.

"Uncle Rob has such a nice lurch," said Mom. "He won the lurching contest in fifth grade, you know. He was the first monster to make the side-ankle lurch popular. Now you see all the zombies doing it."

"You know, Frankie," Mom continued, "you really ought to think about your walk. A good walk can take years to perfect."

"My walk? Can't I just *walk*?"

"Well, you could. But where's the fun in that?

Why walk, when you could STRUT?"

"Mom!" Frankie moaned, clearly
embarrassed. "I don't think so."

"You could PRANCE.
Although, keep in mind that it's hard to look scary while prancing. The best you might hope for is unnerving."

Frankie glanced at the neighboring houses. Was anyone watching? "Really, Mom? Prancing? You can't be serious."

"Serious? Yes, sir!" Mom saluted.

"You could MARCH.

Like they do in the Mermen Corps. Now that can be scary."

"Not scary. Just slimy," said Frankie. "And why would I want to walk like a fish?"

"True. It would be best to use your monster strengths," said Mom.

"You come from a long line of TRUDGERS.

"We Steins are built for it. Aunt Temple was a tap dancer, but she could perform only in theaters with sturdy floors. She could actually bring down the house!"

Frankie gritted her teeth. "Ha. Very funny, Mom."

"Your great-grandfather LUMBERED.

He was half bigfoot, you know," Mom said proudly.

"I don't want to walk like some old bigfoot," said Frankie.

"Then keep trudging in mind.
Get creative with it.

Maybe CLOMP.

It's like trudging with purpose.

Or you could STOMP.

Pretend you're King Kong or Godzilla.
You could make people panic!"

Frankie flinched. "Mom, please don't do that. The neighbors are looking!"

Mom looked over and gave a big smile and a wave. "Oh, the Drakes. They snuck up on me! Vampires are so good at that. They really frighten people.

"You could try that too. It would be unexpected for a Stein to

TIPTOE. Or SNEAK. Or SLINK."

Frankie wondered if she could slink back in the house right now.

"If you really wanted a challenge, you could try to **GLIDE**," said Mom.

"Ghost pageant queens are very good at it. And gliding is very spooky. But it's a lot harder to glide when you don't float."

"I don't want to glide," said Frankie.
"And I have no interest in walking on stage."

Mom pointed at Frankie's feet. "You're lucky you have two legs. You have a lot of options. The monsters with no legs mostly **slither, squirm, or ooze.** Like our neighbor Condi over there.

"If you had four legs, you could **PROWL.**

Like a werewolf. Very creepy."
Mom looked at Frankie.

"You know, if you really want four legs,
we could talk to the doctor about some
adjustments to your arms."

Frankie's jaw dropped. "No!
My arms are just fine, thanks."

"Let's see," Mom said. "What else could you do?

I know! You could **STRIDE**, like your cousin Jason. He wins all those races. Everyone else runs, but he always seems to catch up. That really freaks people out.

"Or maybe you'd like to **MOSEY?**
You mostly see cowboy monsters doing
that. It's really too relaxed to be scary.

"Although," she continued, "I did see
the headless horseman mosey once.
That was horrifying. Hmm. Maybe you
do want to mosey!"

"Mom. Seriously. Stop."

"So, Frankie, do you know what you want to do?"

"I think so," said Frankie.

"You think so? I suspect you have an answer, dear."

"Yes, I know," said Frankie.

"I'm not going to walk at all. I'm going to just stand here like an alien and study you like you're from another planet."

"Oooh. Perfect!" Mom gave Frankie a little hug. "Aliens are terrifying."

About Shades of Meaning

Shades of meaning are the differences that words with the same basic meaning have from one another. Picking just the right word makes your writing and speaking clearer.

EXTRA MEANINGS

This book has a bunch of words that are similar to the word *walk*. *Mosey*, *strut*, and *stride* are all verbs that mean "to walk." But each word has extra meaning that makes it different from the others. *Mosey* means to walk in an unhurried or aimless manner. *Strut* means to walk in a stiff, proud way. *Stride* means to walk with long steps, usually with purpose.

SYNONYMS

Some words have meanings that are even more similar to each other. Synonyms can be exactly the same or almost the same. *Trudge*, *clomp*, and *stomp* all mean to walk heavily. *Trudge* has the added meaning of walking like it's really hard work. *Clomp* means to walk heavily, plus noisily. *Stomp* means to walk heavily and noisily, but usually also angrily.

INTENSITY

Other times, words might mean the same thing, but the intensity is different. One word may be bigger or stronger than another. *Panic, unnerve, creep, spook, frighten, freak out, terrify,* and *horrify* all mean "scare." But you are a lot more scared if you are terrified than if you are simply spooked. The same goes for the words *think, suspect,* and *know* on pages 20 and 21. Knowing is stronger than thinking or suspecting.

You've LEARNED about shades of meaning. You've PICKED UP some new words. You've DISCOVERED how those words are the same but different. Now, what do you want to MASTER next?

Read More

Coffelt, Nancy. *Big, Bigger, Biggest!* New York: Henry Holt and Co., 2009.

Connors, Kathleen. *Synonyms at School.* Word Play. New York: Gareth Stevens Pub., 2013.

Dahl, Michael. *If You Were a Synonym.* Word Fun. Minneapolis: Picture Window Books, 2007.

Heinrichs, Ann. *Synonyms and Antonyms.* Mankato, Minn.: The Child's World, 2011.

Internet Sites

FactHound offers a safe, fun way to find Internet sites related to this book. All of the sites on FactHound have been researched by our staff.

Here's all you do:

Visit **www.facthound.com**

Type in this code: 9781404883208

Check out projects, games and lots more at **www.capstonekids.com**

To Lily, who chose her walk in her own time. – G. M. O.

Dedicated to my parents, who gave me the opportunity to grow up with the monsters of my imagination. – I. S.

Special thanks to our adviser, Terry Flaherty, PhD, Professor of English, Minnesota State University, Mankato, for his expertise.

Editor: Jill Kalz
Designer: Lori Bye
Art Director: Nathan Gassman
Production Specialist: Kathy McColley
The illustrations in this book were created digitally.

Picture Window Books are published by Capstone,
1710 Roe Crest Drive, North Mankato, Minnesota 56003
www.capstonepub.com

Library of Congress Cataloging-in-Publication Data
Olson, Gillia M.
  Monsters can mosey : understanding shades of meaning / By Gillia M. Olson.
     pages cm. — (Nonfiction picture books. Language on the loose.)
  Summary: "Introduces the concept of shades of word meanings through the telling of an original story"—Provided by publisher.
  ISBN 978-1-4048-8320-8 (library binding)
  ISBN 978-1-4795-1919-4 (paperback)
  ISBN 978-1-4795-1906-4 (eBook PDF)
1. English language—Semantics—Juvenile literature. I. Title
PE1583.O47 2014
  428.1—dc23   2013008067

Printed in the United States of America
in North Mankato, Minnesota.
032013   007223CGF13

Look for all the books in the series:

Frog. Frog? Frog!
Understanding Sentence Types

Monsters Can Mosey
Understanding Shades of Meaning

whatever says mark
Knowing and Using Punctuation

When and Why Did the Horse Fly?
Knowing and Using Question Words